Diary of a Broken Vessel

Taylor Barkley

In loving memory of

Edna Mae Fitzpatrick

August 13th, 1922 – February 14th, 2021

You were such a huge part of my heart.

I love you, kiss Grandpa for me.

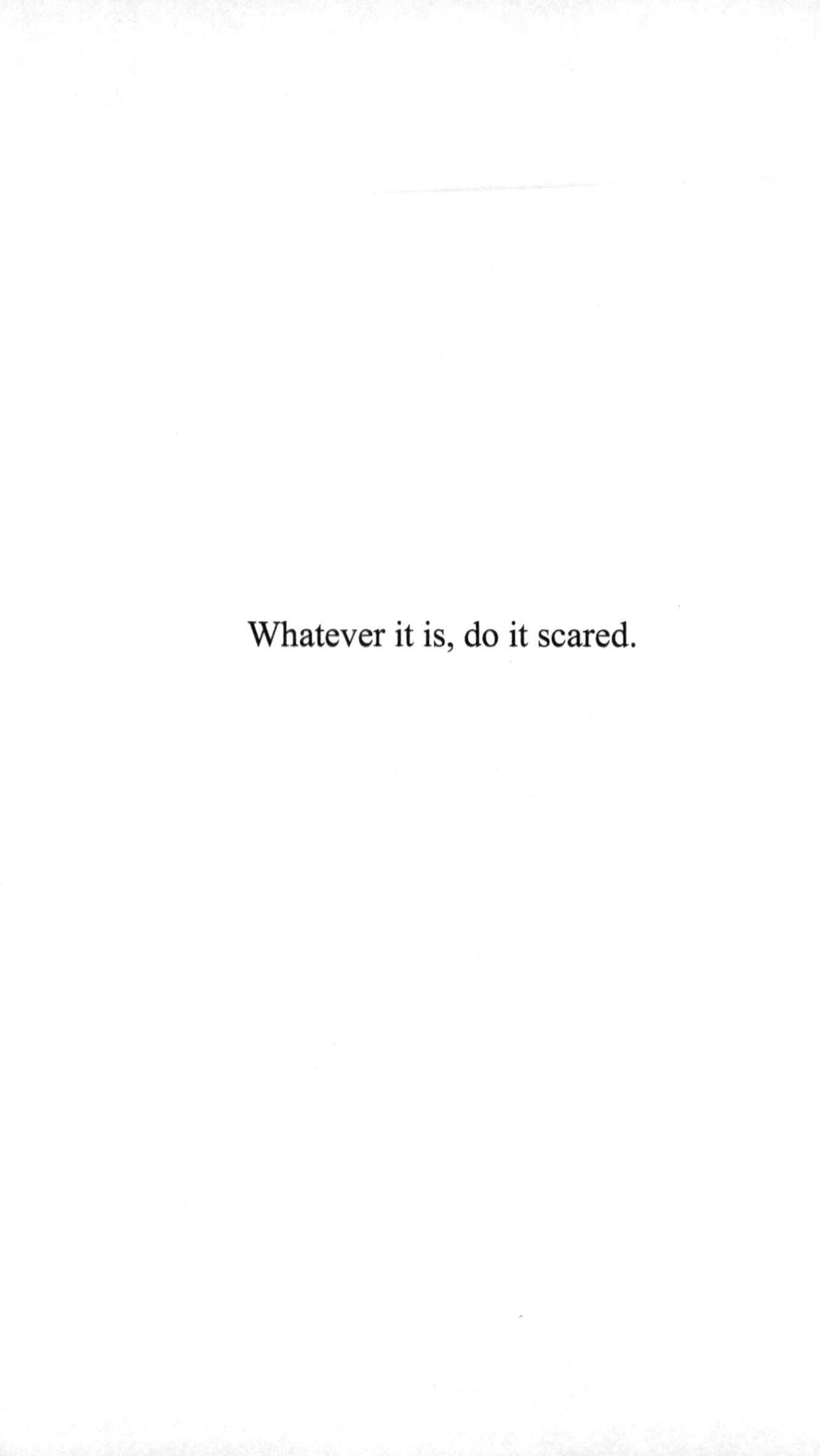

Whatever it is, do it scared.

Special thanks to:

My Heavenly Father.

My community for encouraging me and pointing me back to Christ.

My family for being my sounding boards.

My mommy for reminding me to be unapologetically me.

My bestie, Syd, for the amazing photography and design for the cover.

My cousin, Megan, for being the first to read the draft and helping me iron out the kinks.

Everyone who had to listen to me go back and forth making decisions on details for this project. I needed your listening ears and sound advice.

I love you all more than you know.

Table of Contents

Foreword

Hello there. If you are reading this, first and foremost, thank you for supporting me and this product of a lot of overthinking, prayers, and faith. Why did I decide to put a book out during my final year of undergrad? Who knows? Part of me wanted a tangible collection of my poetry, but in a form in which no one would see it. Weird, right? Another part of me wanted you, who is reading this book, to see a side of me not many people get to see.

That is the essence of who I am as a poet.

My poetry tells a story that I did not think needed to be told. Often, I am mistaken for having it all together because of the way I carry myself. I even bought into that version of me. Somewhere along the way, I decided that would not work for me anymore and that is when the idea for this project evolved. This book became more than just a collection of my poetry, it became about exposing the perfectionist to show the truly broken individual that I am. Some of the poems are light and fun while others are heavier.

This book is me, alive and in print.

The idea to put out this book came from my dad when I was in high school. I never saw myself doing a project of this magnitude, so I politely declined. Long story short, I was scared as one of my close friends pointed out. So, now you hold my fears personified, and an answer to prayers. This book reflects much of which I said I would never do. In fact, my life now is an accurate representation of things I said I would never do.

Let me tell you, God always has the best jokes.

Thank you to my dad for planting the seed, to one of my closest friends, Arielle, for calling me out, and to my Heavenly Father for giving me the courage to do it scared.

Chapter 1

Who am I?

Most of those reading won't know me
But that's okay.
Those who do, have met me in different
chapters of my book of life and only know the
girl they happened to walk in on.
But that's okay.
Because I'll teach you about me
A crash course if you will...

So, allow me to reintroduce myself

I am... the quiet one
with a book in her hand so scared to put it
down because then what will I do with my
hands?

Yes. I can be awkward

Who am I?
I'm the kind of girl who spends all day thinking
about the kind of guy she likes but when
confronted with him she'll say, "he's not my
type."

Who am I?
I am... pardon me... I was the girl who thought her identity lied within a man but then realized that she didn't need a man because she was fearfully and wonderfully created by THE man.

Who am I?
I am the 80's and 90's music lovin, sitcom watchin, natural hair growin, lyrics of poems flowin sista with the tattoos that tell my story and mark my journey through this wave called life. Did I mention I am an old soul?

The one who always feels like she has to have her guard up to block the foolishness that passes for smooth talking these days.

The one who gave her life to Christ but still has doubts because how can a God so perfect love someone so broken who trips over the same hurdle time after time yet still runs back for forgiveness?

Who am I?

I'm the older sister with my brother as my best friend and the heart so big everybody and they mama can fit in it.

I am the one who was afraid to tell her testimony but now shares with the other lost souls about how her crooked sticks can now draw straight lines because of unconditional love. A love outside of the capacity of any man's heart but comes from The One who is a well that never runs dry of grace.

I am the one who went through the fire and lived to tell about it.

I am the redeemed daughter and reborn sister in Christ who stands before you,
A new creation.

I am the girl who now leads from her knees praying to die to herself so that she can love others well. I am not perfect, but I am always progressing.

I am the one who decided to put her heart in a book for all to see the changing power of love and forgiveness.

I am she.
She is me.
Thank you for the opportunity to be
reintroduced.

I Am from Home pt.1

I am from Annagladys Dr.
From Blue's Clues toys
And loud noise.
Garage doors and scrapes on wooden floors
Pots of spaghetti, bowls of salad.
The CD player playing a Merry Christmas
ballad.
I am from preachers and athletes,
Brainiacs and math geeks.
Aaron and Tammy are who I am from
Who always taught me to never play dumb.
I am from Africa, Mexico, Barbados and
Trinidad
All married into one.
One big happy family, that's where I'm from.

I am from Diven Court.
From movers vans and movers trucks.
From farmers markets on the street,
Trying to make a buck.
Amiya and Naomi were born here
To that first day of kindergarten and wiping
away their first tear
From staying up late watching sitcoms
To taking my little brother to his first prom
Old pictures on new walls

New memories made
To gradations and wishing I had stayed
From fireworks and celebrations
Family from different nations.
I am from a family tree
Etched into stone.
I am from a family,
A family from home.

/senˈsāSH(ə)n/

It comes quick
If you blink too long,
You will miss it

A quick rush
Flushing out all thoughts of reason
When you try to focus on it
It goes away
It refuses to hold you for long
So, this is not for the processors
Or the analyzers
Just let it happen
All at once
Or not at all

It comes quick
If you blink too long,
You will miss it

Self-Love

As a small and defenseless child no one told
me how to love myself
However, I was told I was loved, and I was
always reminded of my beauty
But when I looked in the mirror, their
reminders and their love became lost in my
doubt
As a child I knew I didn't know what love was
But I knew doubt, I knew fear, and I knew hurt
As an adolescent I thought loving yourself
meant just saying it with no belief to back it up
My teenage self thought her love for herself
was reflected in how much she bent over
backwards to please others
Loving yourself means believing that you are
the prettiest creation you've ever seen
Look yourself in the mirror and love yourself
enough to tell yourself that you are loved
Allow unconditional love to love you and rest
in its promises
As an adult looking in the mirror covered in
empty words on sticky notes
I want to tell my younger self all the treasures I
have come to find for myself now

*Dear pretty girl... dear beautiful child... dear
masterpiece of a Perfect Creator,
You ARE loved and somewhere along the way
we forget just how precious we are
Putting yourself first doesn't make you selfish.
In fact, it makes you wise
So, love yourself enough to tell the unworthy no
when they ask for pieces of you
Be the prettiest girl you know.
Smile because your joy is hidden behind it
You as a single creation are enough and you
learn to be complete without a man standing by
your side
Dear beautiful brown eyed child, love yourself
enough not to give pieces of you away to boys
who know not of your value.
Those pieces add up and you won't find
yourself in subtracting but in adding space for
God to live in your heart.*

You are loved.

This is a poem for me

The me that I am falling more in love with
the me that my Heavenly Father spent so much
time crafting and creating
This poem is for the beautifully broken,
flawed individual that is Taylor C.
Or Ms. Barkley if ya nasty
This poem is to appreciate the one that
constantly gets forgotten by my own self
So, you are excused while I celebrate me
It was once said by an illustrious woman
herself
That to love yourself means loving the God
who created you
Loving me means appreciating me for all the
stretch marks, bumps, and bruises
The sometimes-clear skin
And the tummy that will not go away
Loving me means all of me
The good me
The bad me
All. of. me.
From my dark brown crown of tight curls
to my pretty pedicured toes
Self-love equals the best love
And it is way past due,
but don't worry I'm almost finished

Loving me means not being afraid to look
myself in the mirror and remind me of my
dopeness
It's wearing what I want to wear because I like
it
And not to fit into a box of who you think I'm
supposed to be
Loving me is treasuring the element of surprise
when men think I am incapable of keeping
them so weak in the knees they can hardly
speak.
To love The Creator means
that I cannot withhold any amount of love from
myself
I must love me well
For I know that I AM fearfully and wonderfully
made.
My father never makes mistakes
Which means that I am his version of perfect
and he loves every inch of me

And so will I.

Blessed Assurance

The smell of crimson roses
And fresh rain fills my nose
As you are cried over, prayed over,
But for some reason I cannot cry, I cannot pray.
I can only think
Who will sit in your chair in the den?
Who will beat all your grandchildren in
Monopoly?
Who will pray over dinner for Thanksgiving,
Christmas, and Easter?
Am I selfish to think of these things?
To think not about how you are no longer in
pain
Or not that your wife of over 60 years
Has now lost a husband and a father to your
children
Maybe I am selfish
I close my eyes as they wrap your flag
And as the seven men line up in the grass to
take their shots,
I turn away.
My eyes mist and my heart sinks
I know I must be selfish
So, as we gather in your home

Before we start to eat, I realize
That nothing will ever be the same
My dad will pray over dinner for Thanksgiving,
Christmas, and Easter
Your oldest son will become the champion in
Monopoly
And everyone will sit in your chair

First Homecoming

Seeing you for the first time in a while was...
different
We both knew it was
You rushed in to greet me, eager to embrace
But even your bubbling excitement couldn't
mask the feeling that things had changed
Hugging you felt like hugging a thin and frail
ghost
Stepping into the house felt... different
Finally being able to see the chipped paint on
the walls that had always been there was
shocking
On the outside the foundation doesn't appear to
have changed
But in coming home, one thing was made
painfully clear
Everything done in the dark will come to light
From the chipped paint to the dirty carpet
To the couch stains
Every crack in the foundation is made painfully
clear
But you and I talk as if we don't hear the
creaking floors that hold late night arguments
Or the closed doors hiding holes in the walls

How could I have missed the damage?
Seeing what used to be home in rose-colored
glasses will do that to you
But winter has sprung
So there's no need for sunglasses
And everything is made clear
On display for all who are willing to pay
attention
If only these dirty walls could talk
Or the carpets ripped up to reveal what's really
been hiding under there.
Gone are the days of Saturday morning
cartoons and biscuits on the way to church on
Sunday's
Goodbye to the joint conversations and warmth
of laughter
To being the loudest at every choir
performance, every play, and every track meet.
Getting older and coming home things aren't
always as they once seemed to be
You can grow up in the same house
But experience two different versions of your
parents
Four became three

And familiar became unrecognizable.

I know I've been changed.

If only you knew the story

What God's grace has covered me for

What His grace has brought me through.

WHEW CHILE this is long overdue.

But right on time

The mountains in my mind

Self says to herself
How did we end up back here?
Back to the edge of the cliff we pushed
ourselves to.
More importantly, how do I get back down?
How do I free myself from the thoughts that
almost push me over the edge every time?
Day in and day out
Sometimes the truth is enough to anchor me
But other days truth is like an old raggedy
umbrella
Incapable of shielding me from the heavy gusts
of wind that blow me away
Everything I thought I knew
Goes away with the wind too
The truth shall set us free
But is that even a possibility for us?
Our mind works like the speed of light and
Our thoughts and truth are like oil and water
One always rejecting the other
Finding no common ground to stand on
And that's how we ended up here
At the cliff
With no way of coming down

Are we weak?

Or just weary of always having to lower our
blood pressure
When lies come to raise it right back up again
We've been to this cliff so many times that our
footprints look like they belong here

Self says to herself again
It's okay,
We can make it back to where our surroundings
are familiar
We can make it off this cliff
Truth can be louder than lies
But only if we allow it to be.

For the sake of poetry

Sitting down and leaving it all

Where you are

Just for the sake of a poem

Is hard

My mind wanders around the block finding
things to write about

But skipping the things I care most about

Because a poem must be about a certain thing

For the sake of poetry

****

What even is poetry?

Is it putting emphasis on words and putting
yourself in other settings?

Is it speaking from the heart or dissecting the
mind for a greater purpose?

The journey of a writer

Is one not native to everyone

You question yourself a lot

But one thing I did not expect in this particular passion

Was the evidence of comparison

For a while wanting to be a "good poet" choked me up and stunted my growth

Walking around voiceless as a proclaimed writer portrays you as misguided or uninspired

When it turns out… I was just… scared.

Scared of what my voice would sound like on paper

Scared that my voice would sound like a squeaking toy

Obnoxious... not needed.

But for the sake of all things creative and creatively sound

Your voice holds your freedom

So, ring the bell

For the sake of all thing's poetry

Chapter II

I am from home part 2.

Being from these collections of home mean
everything to me
However, the need to explore deeper into who I
am comes from the lack of that awareness in
my own education
Until nourished,
My lack of knowledge runs dry
So, who am I?
Who are my people?
I am a descendant of my blend of culture
Evenly distributed of island girl and
Indigenous people
I am from where
Rhythm and blues are baked into every dialect
and gospel song
And soul is always on the menu
I'm always in a family I've never biologically
belonged to
But that's the beauty of where I'm from
Hearing the terms baby girl and sweetheart like
they came from my own parents
This is how my people are
Where everyone is indirectly the descendant of
somebody great
Aunties and uncles spoil you at the expense of
themselves

And ma dukes always adds that extra to
everything she makes
Record players on low
Spades games escalating
Sitcoms playing as white noise
Line dancing tying it all together
For we know a gathering isn't made until
somebody puts on the Al Green or Frankie
Beverly records
It's a whole different world out here
One where you are either Living Single or In
Living Color
Full of melanin or lacking in it
Family Matters where I come from
From the dashikis
And vibrantly colored head wraps
To black panther mantras and faded
photographs
All telling a story
A story of where I'm from
I am from a family
I am from home.

L.O.V.E

Love
is telling me when my butt is too big in a pair
of jeans or telling me when I am talking too
much.

Love
is finding someone who completes me, matches
me, and makes me feel loved.

Love
is telling me you like me for who I am but of
course I have to doubt you because that's what
girls do right?

Love
is the little things that make me smile
like coming home to a clean house and cooked
dinner or "just because" flowers at work.

Love
is red roses with anniversary dinners
and impromptu dance parties in the kitchen.

Love
is being with the man I lost my heart to,
and signing up to grow old and grey like a
timeless romance film.

Love
is sticking around and dodging the broken
dishes against the wall and the bullets that
that pierced your soul.

Love
is being the things I never knew to ask for and
being what I never knew I needed.

Love
isn't the superficial and perfect posts that
everyone makes for our viewing pleasure. is
love only the highlights? is love a feeling? is it
lasting? does it hurt? instead, pull back the
dysfunction that society glorifies to reveal
authentic and real love.
because the reality is

Love
isn't perfect. it takes more work than what is
shown in pretty pictures.
if the propaganda matched the behind the
scenes, nobody would buy it.

Love
isn't toxic, but it does require death.
death to the selfish beings we are for the
sake of the one who is undeserving.

Love
isn't love until it is tested with the
unconditional.
what good does it do you to keep it all to
yourself? it must be tested by fire to come out
pure.

Love
is being able to see me for me. see me for all
the flaws and scars and still choose me. love
isn't always the warm and fuzzy,
but the grace and sacrifice that it requires.

Love
is sacrificial, patient, forgiving, longsuffering, overwhelming,
virtuous, and everlasting. it isn't toxic, fake, or for show.

L.O.V.E.

Hell Hath No Fury

They say a woman with a plan, a prayer and a
made-up mind is dangerous...
But what about a woman living her life on
mission?
Clinging to celibacy
Searching soul satisfaction
Constantly minimizing herself
So that only her creator can be seen?
Is she dangerous?
Does her inquisitiveness attract you?
Does her burning light blind you?
Given the circumstances of her life the
previous quote should permanently be changed.
Altered to reflect the road she is on and the
goals she sets
So instead of a prayer, a made-up mind, and a
plan
Let's make a dangerous woman out of a soul, a
passion to know HIM, and an ultimate goal.
Now that woman?
Don't get in her way.

Aftermath

Breathe in

Everything stills around me
As if for a brief second you can pause nature
I blink away tears and
The visions of you go away with them
Every time I blink
The almost emerald green of the pastures in
front of me become clearer

Breathe out

I was told to come here and find my peace
The peace you were supposed to be for me
The tears threaten to overflow now, and I can't
blink fast enough to keep them away
Everything here reminds me of you
The wind forcing to push me whichever way it
blows
Swaying me in and out unsure of where it
wants me
The clouds covering the sun one minute
Bringing a shadow over the surface
And then giving way to its shine the next
My cold fingers are the only thing not warmed
by the sunshine

Breathe in

It's too still here
It's not what I'm used to
But yet I feel your presence around me
It's what makes me stay
The wind blowing my hair feels like fingertips
on my scalp
Your fingertips

Breathe out

I came here to get you out of my system
So I could stop seeing you
Feeling like you're always there
But I guess you will always be there
Tethered to my soul somehow
So no matter what I do
Or where I go
You'll always be there.

21.

What has become of me?
What is becoming of me?
In the 7,300 and now 7,301 days that I have
been on this planet what has become of me?
Well, at 5"5 I stand with the boldness to say
that
I am just happy to be alive
Of all the lessons I have learned
And places I've been
There is still so much more
More to soak in
More to discover
I was blessed with a beautiful mind
That I use to ponder how in the world I made it
this far.
I have beat most statistics
And outrun the limits others have set for me
And even the limits I put on myself
I dream big
And think even bigger
But most importantly
I love
I have been loved

Freely grace has been given to me
For me to freely give to others
And mercy's spared
See...of all the things I've learned
One thing has truly set me free
The weight of its knowledge is what keeps me
free
And it is that
There is no place I can go
No valley too deep
No mountain too high
Where I can outrun his love
No matter how many times I pull away from it
Or reject it
Or even refuse to show others the same kind of
love
I will still always be covered
And that red looks real good on me

Always Remember

Here are a few things to remember
Tips for the road
Keep them close and tuck them away
Hide them in your heart where they are left guarded.
To forget is to have forsaken a very piece of you.

The way to a man's heart is always through his stomach so pay attention to mama in the kitchen now chile.

Season your food with salt and that extra that only you can give.

Always remember that what goes around comes around and one will always reap what they sow.

Therefore, sow seeds of love and unconditional grace and you will always find yourself at its knees.

Remember that joy and happiness are not synonymous.

Joy is the feeling of knowing that absolutely everything is under the control of the one who took the time to create you.
It is not fleeting nor is it reliant on another creation.

Happiness is fleeting and as unreliable as a wobbly ladder.
One moment it may hold you up, and in the next moment it collapses.

Prayer and a little bit of faith changes everything
And out of the heart the mouth speaks so be careful what you say to others.

Always remember to keep enough money in a separate place in case of a rainy day.

You never want to borrow more than you are able to pay back.

Remember that flour always gets rid of grease fires and vinegar kills gnats.

Remember that love is both a choice and a command and in order to love others you must love yourself as much as the Creator loves you.

Pain is fleeting. It may last for a night, or a few nights.

The joy always comes, but peace may come first.

Always remember who you are when no one is watching defines the character you will be when someone is.

And that absolutely no one likes a liar.

Your strength lies deeper than you think and sometimes needs a push to reach the surface.

And lastly remember this very thing,

You, and every single element about you, matters. You are more than enough and your role in God's plan never changes and neither does His love for you.

Always remember that.

Dear White People

This isn't your typical "dear white people" poem
full of things the majority shouldn't do towards
me the double minority.
Well sort of...
This is an appeal to the white people who have
asked me questions.
I welcome inquiries about my hair and about my
experience as an African American woman.
This is to give you as many answers as possible.

Dear White People, peep this. If I come in one
day with a hairstyle that is peculiar to you, I'd
like for you to ask me before you just assume
you can touch it.
Yes, it is 9 times out of 10 not my own hair.
But if I bought it, it's mine.
Yes, I also wear my natural hair out
However, as you see, it's a lot of hair and it's not
as easily manageable as yours... which is why I
wear weave.

Dear White People, I believe that education is the gateway to freedom of the mind. So please, when you ask me your questions, know that I as one black woman do NOT speak for all black women. I am responsible for my own experience and the knowledge that I on my own have attained. If your quest for knowledge is valid then ask freely. If you ask only to reaffirm the stereotypes you have already placed on me... keep your questions to yourself, respectfully.

Dear White People, when racism and modern-day lynching's fill the media and the climate of the country proves yet again the little value on black lives... check you privilege at the door. Know that you will never truly understand what it means to be black in America. If you are vexed by what you see... become an ally. Speak out about injustices, but from the ally's point of view. Educate your friends who may be racist, and fact check before you run off at the mouth.

Dear White People, I acknowledge that to be black in America is both a burden and a blessing. Our style fuels popular culture and all though it's trending... it's not yours to appropriate or capitalize off of. Before you tell me you wish your skin was as brown as mine, stop and think about what that means. Being brown or black means stepping into the full embodiment of our struggles, our hindrances, our history, and our pain. Is that what you want for yourself?
I didn't think so.

In conclusion,
Appreciate but don't appropriate
Look but don't touch
Admire but don't loathe
Think before you speak
Right is right, wrong is wrong, and racism isn't a topic to agree to disagree on.
There is no gray area when it comes to the value of a black life.
Dear White People

focus...

settle down and be still

breathe in

take that breath

down to the core

hold it there

focus...

concentrate on

the warming of the sun

and the serenity of peace

as it rules over hearts and minds

focus...

on how worries

seem to melt away

like tension on relaxed muscles

focus...

on the shimmering

of your skin

in the sweltering sun

like it was always supposed

to be exposed to it

or the magic of melanin turning to gold

no matter the shade

focus…

settle down and be still

breathe in

take that breath

down to the core

hold it there

Midnight

Sometimes I wish I could embrace you
To lay up under you while
You trace circles on my thighs
And politely sniff my hair
I feel safe with you
Arms around me
Pulling me into safety
Legs and arms intertwined
So that between the two of us there is no
beginning and no end
It's moments like this
Where I feel true bliss
And I know it's wrong
To be here with you
Skin caressing each other
Hearts beating in tandem
I know it's wrong
But how could something that feels
So secure
So amazing
Be so wrong?
The reality sets in like the setting sun
But if we don't move
Maybe we won't see it
The conviction in my stomach starts to fade
I know I'm in trouble with God

I can hear thunder rolling outside
So, I close my eyes
And burrow closer into your chest
So that I am intoxicated by your scent
Don't think about it and you'll be okay

Refined

Who do you think I am?
What do I look like to you?
I must not mean that much for you to really
believe that after all this time I'd still accept the
same stuff
I must not be like the queen you were once
dating.
Why think so highly of her and not of me?
I must not be the true daughter of the God in
heaven that you claim to worship and serve on
social media.
Nah... I must not be like any of that to you.
Instead I'm the second choice
I'm the dirty secret that you can delete when
your girl checks your phone
Or erase along with our past messages
I'm that to you.

I never cried over you... until now
Never cried when I saw on Instagram you had
snagged the attention of a beautiful chocolate
queen.
Never cried when you continuously put me out
of your life because of her.

I'm much better than that
So, because of that, I will not bad mouth you or
her
Because I know who I am
I added up my worth and added tax and then it
hit me
That you continuously showed me that you
came up insufficient
For even 25% of my total value
I know better
So now those who know better, must do better
But I will say, I did cry when I realized that I'm
not the same broken and perverted little girl
that you had fun with every now and then
I cried when I realized that you still expected
me to be around hanging onto every message
you ever sent me
And the lack of appreciation you showed for
what I had to offer
I cried when I realized that the God I serve
looked at me in a way you never could
He saw beauty in who I was and decided
To take me through the fire and show me that I
was made for better
Deserved better

Now here we are

Me crying... not over you... but for you
I cry because I pray you know the true love of
my God
Because once you do you will think twice
before settling for less and for making another
queen feel cheap
You will know that you deserve better than
what you feel you must overcompensate for
You will be better
And do better
So yes... I cried for you.
But most of all I cried over all the pieces finally
coming together
I cried over who I once was.
Emphasis on was.
Because I am not that girl anymore
So again, I ask you
Who do you think I am?
What do I look like to you now?

unknown

Isn't this how you're supposed to feel?
Heart matching the rhythm of what it hears
Pulse steadying
Body slowly responding to what enters its ear
gates
Breathing slows
Eyes close
Isn't this how you're supposed to feel?
Waves of intense calmness
Wash over my body
And
It
Brings
Me
Peace
Deep breaths taken in and pushed
Down to my core
Then out
Everything feels smooth
Smooth like velvet under fingertips
Or silk on skin
I think I am relaxed now
Nothing exists outside of this moment
Then it ends

Chapter III

I choose you

This wasn't always a thing
You were just a figment of my imagination
You were in the songs I digested
And in verses spoken over me
I didn't even know you were an option
My current choices consisted of filling my life
with poison
Appealing to the eye but ignoring the skull and
crossbones on the back of the label
Freely running back every time I needed a pick
me up
Or to relieve a little stress.
I was comfortable in my choices
Numb to how they were really affecting me
Until you came along
You offered me freedom
Freedom wrapped tightly in grace and stamped
with mercy
It seemed too good to be true
Like the cure to cancer
Or an end to racism
So, no wonder why I was skeptical

Even when I felt forced
You reminded me that the choice was always
mine to make
So, I took my time
Put it on the shelf
Picked it up every now and then
I even tried the free 30-day option
You know when you buy something, wear it out,
and send it back in hopes of a refund
But unbeknownst to me it was something my
spirit actually liked
I caught a glimpse of what life would be like
with it
And that...sold me
So, I chose you
With no guarantee that you would make good on
the promises you spoke of
But I chose you anyway
And now... more than ever I know I made the
right choice
There was no buyer's remorse this time
You were perfect for me
Your sacrifice is what rid my life of poison
Making me as promising as

A sunrise on a new day.

So, I choose you
Now and forever
I choose you
When all hell breaks loose, and Satan wants to
grab my hand
I choose you
When the fear of the future chokes me up
And my worries are like paperweights on my
mind
Or even when my past threatens to be the hurdles
I'll never get over
I choose you
Now and forever
I choose you

{the power of the poet}

> to educate and entertain
> through words
> cleverly strung
> together using
> comparisons and
> personification
>
> to express ourselves
> through bold claims
> convicting tones
> seductive lyrics with
> the intention to open
> our brains and expose
> our souls to you the
> consumer
>
> to challenge
> and awaken forward
> thinkers, believers, and
> dreamers. to open
> your eyes beyond the
> tunnel you see through
> all while inserting
> pieces of ourselves
> and incorporating our

truths and vernacular
that both excites you
and speaks to you.

and that's dope

Real Thing

You satisfy me
Here I sit
With a chill to my bones
Desperate to just feel the warmth
Of your presence
You are the only thing that matters now
Melodies sing around me
And here I sit
Desperate
Longing
To feel your presence
I would trade thousands of these days
For one day
One touch by you
I would trade a thousand
Oh I've tasted and I've seen
The sweetness of your love
The goodness of your grace
So here I sit
Desperate
Longing
To feel the warmth of the sun
As if it is you wrapping me in your arms

Behind my eyes
I see you
Holding my face in your bruised hands
Catching every tear
Behind my eyes I see you gazing lovingly
Into my soul
Behind my eyes I see you
Holding my hand with the grip of a thousand
promises
I know you won't ever let go
Behind my eyes I know you see me
Right where I am
Holding onto my heart

So here I sit
Desperate
Longing
Wishing to be dismissed into eternity with you
I am done pretending to be okay without you
I am done singing you lies
I am done pushing your sacrifice away
I have tasted and seen of the sweetest love
This is the real thing

A mother's love

I remember I used to come into your bedroom
every morning before being sent off to school

Just to lay next to you and get those few extra
minutes of sleep and soak in the warmth
radiating from your body

"Good morning Mommy"

"Good morning Taylor"

Then closing my eyes until dad came in to pray
with us before shuffling off to school

This was our routine

The best way to start my day

I remember our conversations growing up

I wanted to do everything you did

Even when we would fight

I couldn't escape the truth of our similarity

I look just like you

My fight for individuality

Clouded the beauty that comes from a mother's love

Loving you came with understanding you

It was as if the blindfold of ignorance fell like dead skin

I could see your tenderness

Your unique capacity for love

All wrapped in the warmth of your hug

The way you empathize and want to be seen is like my own

It was undeniable; so I stopped running.

a haiku a day...

Romans 1:16
Set free from guilt and shame
Living unashamed

a haiku a day…

59

The revolution
Will not be televised
Don't stay asleep

a haiku a day...

When the sun rises
Joy is the promise of day
Yet the pain remains

a haiku a day...

61

Brown the color
The color of coffee and
Cream make the color of me

a haiku a day...

62

They love my culture
They see me as a threat
How to love them well?

a haiku a day…

*The story I'll tell
I don't look like what I've done
The story I'll tell*

a haiku a day...

Find your home away
From home. The place you find rest
Home is where you are

a haiku a day...

I know to trust you
My anchor to the ground
He'll never let me go

a haiku a day...

Being a poet
For the sake of poetry
Write until you are free

self-con·fi·dence

she believed she could, so she did

she knew the risks

calculated from every angle

and still she did

after she was done

she took a step back admiring her

masterpiece

and she was glad she did.

Good Morning

Feet padding down the tile hallway

I look into the light at the end of my tunnel vision

Here sits an elegant view

Here is where I find my equilibrium

The serene and peaceful spot by the window is slightly disturbed by the tiny sound of Stevie Wonder blasting through headphones

The occasional sound here and there

Pale in comparison to the landscape view of the outside

Orange and green leaves creep from one side of the window, hanging from a twisty tree

Threatening to obstruct the whole view

But they don't

Instead they hold back the rays of sun starting to rise

The silent song of sunrise comes to a climax

As the normal bustle of the morning gives way

Good Morning.

Students go from here to there, trying to get to class on time,

But me?

I sit in the serene and peaceful spot by the window.

The Lord's Prayer

Our Father, my father, which art in heaven,
Hallowed be thy Name.
A name that is above any other name
And at times when I get so wrapped up in my
selfish thoughts... the power of your name has
and will always stay the same.
Thy Kingdom come.
Thy will be done on earth,
As it is in heaven.
May you guide me to stay in the will that is
divine and let me not run too far that I pass the
sign and end up crossing the line into the
permissive.
Give us this day our daily bread.
As it is nourishment to my spirit and
strengthening to my bones.
Forgive us of our trespasses,
As we forgive them that trespass against us
And lead us not into temptation,
Forgive me, Father for I sin every day.
I sing you lies on Sundays,

Continue in nasty habits on Mondays,
Pull it together for bible study on Tuesdays,
Fall into sexual sin on Wednesdays,
Cuss a customer out on Thursdays,
Allow stress to pressure me on Fridays,
and sleep all day Saturdays.
For I am unworthy of your reckless and
unwavering love.
Help me to learn to let go of past hurts, and
pain, and heal those cuts so deep that they have
damaged major organs
But deliver us from evil.
For thine is the kingdom,
The power, and the glory,
For ever and ever.
Amen.

Triggered

What happens when you are triggered?

For me, everything in my body tenses.

I stop breathing for a second. If I was in a movie, this is the scene where everything stops while a single moment is replayed in my eyes.

That is where I would be.

Beware of your triggers they say.

Eliminate those things that trigger you.

How do I eliminate the way my skin feels when it receives a warm hug? How do I eliminate my vivid dreams? Because the reality is, you never know when a trigger is coming, or how long it will last.

It is like a contraction, overtaking all of you at once. Eliminating the outside world and holding you captive until it is over.

Truth is… even in our surprisingly brief time together, there are too many of those memories to eliminate.

The way you still smelled good after a stressful workday…

The way you swept me in with those bear-like but affectionate hugs…

The security I felt in those moments…

The way you examined my outfit and the Starbucks we went to…

The mint tea you ordered and the park you walked me to after…

The small fight we had and the kiss that made it all better…

The silent slow dance we shared under the leaves and the spontaneity of it all…

I cannot eliminate those.

Triggered

Wishin

Going through life wishin that the way things are
Could be reversed
I wish I knew that the bed on the other side
Was laced with fire and pain and passion
dripping in fears and tears
And heartache
Wishin that on the eve of my 6th month anniversary
I wouldn't have to look forward to such a milestone
Wishin I'd never made the list
Checked it twice
Wishin that making it through the day wouldn't be what I look forward to
Wishin I found my worth wrapped in the love of Jesus instead of the arms of a man
Wishin one man wouldn't have made that mistake with me
Wishin that my mistakes wouldn't come back to collect
Because I ran up the check and now the bill is due
Wishin that the nights where I cry silent tears
Squeezing my legs closed just so I can sleep with some kind of peace

Never existed
I wish I could take it all back
21 for 21 and I'm paying the price
This kind of experience
Is like no other
I'm not tryna hear it will get better
Because I want it to be gone
Wishin

Worth the Wait

You are worth the wait

You are worth being sought after, loved on, and
pursued
Though your past may haunt you like the souls
of dead ancestors

You are worth the wait

You are worth what it may take to peel back the
layers to reveal your true essence
You are worth the tireless pursuit of your heart
You are worth what it may take to finally reach
you
The booby traps
The broken glass
The trap doors
The smoke and mirrors
All worth trudging through to get to you
The real you
The one who sits in the corner hiding hoping to
never be hurt like that again
The seasons of reopened wounds and tearful
nights

The seasons of embracing being physically
alone for the sake of your healing and serenity

All worth it
Because you, my darling

Are worth the wait

Hey there,

You have reached the end of my journey as a writer. Before you go, I wanted to share my story with you. My "why." I hesitated on the decision to put my story in my first book. As I thought about it more, I decided that since my poetry shows a side of me that not most get to see, my story belonged in this book. My prayer is that whoever reads this would find themselves in what I have been through and what it took to get here. I pray that God uses my experience to truly change those who hear it and in return draw them closer to Him.

It is not a pretty story... but it is one that needs to be told.

I was blessed to grow up in a loving household with two parents and a younger brother. Although we were not perfect by any means, I know that a two parent Christian household is not as common. Both of my parents were deacons at my church so that meant I never missed a Sunday and I also had my own responsibilities at church. Although I seemed like a blessed child, my experiences begged to differ.

I was molested twice around the ages of six or seven by someone I trusted. This event opened the doors to a pattern of sexual abuse in my life. **It also began what could be one of the biggest lessons in forgiveness that I would ever learn.** My views of God and true love were damaged, and it has taken half of my life to heal from what broke me. Growing up, I was painfully shy with not many friends. I was bullied for being the quiet one and the good girl. After being sexually assaulted by an 8th grader when I was in the 6th grade, I started to rebel against that "good girl" image. At the Christian school I went to, we were taught about God. However, at that point in my life I could not see how a perfect and loving God could let so many traumatizing things happen to someone he said he loved. I was carrying around a heavy load of hurt and anger and felt I had every right to be resentful of God.

Highschool for me was not horrible because I chose to get involved in extracurricular activities. On the outside I was fine, but inside I was struggling with my loneliness, lack of self-esteem, and self-worth. I was still introverted and my relationship with God only existed on Sunday mornings at church. I had only one close friend and I never trusted her with the knowledge of anything I was struggling with out of fear of judgement. I was struggling with pornography and masturbation until I became sexually active my senior year of high school. I knew that I was supposed to wait to have sex until marriage because it was the "Christian thing to do," but I was not interested in obeying any of Gods laws. I was living a double life full of lies, deceit, and at the end of the day, pain.

When I got to college, I wanted to continue to live the life I was living and exercise my freedom, so I continued to sleep around. I was hoping to find love or a sense of worth in whoever I was with. I was only satisfying my flesh until I was left with my depression and loneliness. There was a campus ministry that my best friend told me about, called the Neo Impact Movement. After attending one meeting, I was greeted with so much love from the students that it scared me. I was not used to people being so nice without having an agenda, and I never had real and authentic friendships with anyone that I was not sleeping with. I was certain that the people of Impact were crazy and only wanted to get close to me to eventually hurt or take advantage of me. After a while, my depression became unbearable and the one thing that I would use to cope was no longer helping me. **Unbeknownst to me, God was working on my heart and wanted me to realize that he was the only thing that could heal my hurt and truly satisfy me.**

Remember that lesson in forgiveness I was telling you about? Here it is...

One of the things that God calls us to do as Christians is to forgive. *"Make allowance for each other's faults and forgive anyone who offends you. Remember, the Lord forgave you, so you must forgive others" {Colossians 3:13}.* For most of my childhood, I wrestled with my anger for those who took advantage of me and refused to forgive. I did not feel like they deserved to be forgiven. As I came to know who Christ was for myself, I was able to forgive the boy in the 8th grade and the person who molested me and started this whole thing. I realized that forgiveness is a choice and not a magical feeling. It was a choice I made for my own health and in order to have a relationship with the person who hurt me. The love that I have for that person was enough to forgive them and for me to let go of my anger. To this day, we are very close and the reality of God's unconditional love for me through Jesus has helped me show them the same love. It is not easy but forgiving them is a constant reminder of the forgiveness that I have in Jesus. It also helps to bring them closer to God and closer to forgiving themselves for the mistake they made.

It took me going through all that pain, and years of self-medicating with sex to turn me to the unconditional love and forgiveness that God was showing me. I rejected it for so long because I thought I already knew what love was by what I had been shown on this earth. I learned that when I am angry, I can give that to God even if it is him I am mad at. For a while, I blamed God for allowing those men to hurt me. I blamed him for all the times I turned away from him and tried to fill that hole in my heart with everything but him. But the more I learned about who God was, the more I realized the power in my story. With all this knowledge, I was able to forgive those who had abused me because I know I had been forgiven for all the times I cheated on God. Now when I see the man who started all of this, I do not see the mistake he made in hurting me. I see him as one of God's children. **That is the power of forgiveness.** When I finally stopped trying to outrun God's love and embraced it, it made it easier to show that love to others. He still loved and pursued me even when I wanted nothing to do with him. Those nights I spent in my dorm room crying because I felt so alone, he was there. He heard my cries and sent amazing friends to further show me how much he truly loves me.

My college career has not been easy and there were many times my faith was tested. Like the time where I was almost kicked out of classes mid semester, or not being able to start classes until after the first week, or when I was sexually assaulted (again) by a guy I was dating my junior year of college. After all I have been through just on this campus alone, most would question why I still follow Christ or why I do not look like what I have been through. I am here to tell you, that through all the sexual abuse and pain from childhood to now, God has consistently shown me why my story is not just for me. Bad things happen because we are all broken people living in a fallen world. However, God has used what I have been through and the broken parts of my story to help others and in return, heal me.

Today, I can tell you that I am in a season of healing and celibacy through counseling and my community. Some days are better than others and every day I must make a conscious decision to allow God to heal what I have kept hidden. I am truly grateful for Impact and the relationships I have made through this movement. I could not have prayed for the kind of friends I have now. Without them I would not be here sharing my testimony, or even serving with Impact. They point me back to Christ, hold me accountable, and sometimes roll up at my apartment when I try to stay isolated.

If you do not listen to any parts of my story, I plead with you, please take away this one thing.

Know that no matter what happened to you in the past, there is still hope for you. You are not too broken or too damaged that the one and true living God cannot use you to reach others. He takes your brokenness and uses that for your good and ultimately for his glory. God uses crooked sticks to make straight lines. Nothing on this earth can separate you from his love, and no matter how far you run he is always pursuing you with love. I used to think that after everything I have done, he would never even want to call me his child. That is why there is GRACE. Know that what happened to you is not your fault but that the choice to forgive and heal is your responsibility.

Romans 8:28 says "And we know that God causes everything to work together for the good of those who love God and are called according to his purpose for them". This means he takes the good, the bad, and the ugly. Because of this he has used me and everything I went through to shape me into the person that I am today.

Thank you from the bottom of my heart for purchasing my book. Thank you for indulging me as I shared with you a very personal part of me through my poetry and through my story. Thank you for allowing me to exercise my voice as a writer. My prayer is that you took something away from this book. Feel free to share with someone who needs to hear it just as much as you did. I would love to hear about which poem you loved the most.

Feel free to reach out to me via Instagram (@taykor__) or by email (taylorbarkley2020@gmail.com).

Until next time.

About the Author

Taylor Barkley is a 5th year college student at Kent State University. She is graduating in August of 2021 with a bachelor's degree in Educational Studies with a minor in Pan-African Studies. She has hopes of incorporating her passions of ministry and education into a career someday. Outside of writing she enjoys other creative hobbies such as painting.

Her love for writing came from her dad and it is her form of release. Discovering her voice as a writer was a huge hurdle that she now feels has been cleared with the release of her first book. Her hope is that through her decision to write unapologetically, someone can relate and find the courage to do the same.